†HE
MOMEN†

†HE MOMEN†

POETRY FOR THE SOUL

GREG E. STEPPES

Tandem Light Press

Tandem Light Press
950 Herrington Road
Suite C128
Lawrenceville, GA 30044

Tandem Light Press paperback edition October 2016

ISBN: 978-0-9976797-4-8
Library of Congress Control Number: 2016954119

PRINTED IN THE UNITED STATES OF AMERICA

CONTENTS

CONTENTS

DEDICATION

To my parents... Gloria and Ted Steppes.
There are no words to describe you. You were truly heaven sent.
Thank you for everything. Thank you for the love, the teaching, the
training, and with God's help, for the man I am today. I will always
love you. I miss you, and I will always be the man that you and God
all want me to be.

Love always, your son, Greg.

ACKNOWLEDGMENTS

First and foremost, I would like to thank God for making this book
possible. I thank my best friends, Pam Freeman, Kristy Stringfellow,
and Tymeeka Carter for all of their support. I thank my godchildren
Ronald, India, Toya, Sierra, and Melissa for the inspiration. And I
thank the lady of my life, Gail.

THAT WOMAN IS A SUCCESS

Who loves life
and lives it to the fullest.
Who has discovered and shared
the strengths and talents
that are uniquely her own.

Who put her best into each situation
better than she found it.
Who seeks and finds that which
is beautiful in all people and all things.
Whose heart is full of love
and warm with compassion.

Who has found joy in living
and peace with in herself.
And who is different from
everybody else.

A BEAUTIFUL ANGEL

When I met you
I said, "Lord, could this be true?
A beautiful angel
right in my view?"

When I look around,
oh what do I see?
A beautiful angel
looking at me.

Your smile brightens the earth,
and your love calms the sea.
I can't explain
what you do to me.

Yes, heaven is missing an angel.
It's sad but true.
For the angel I'm speaking of
is you.

JUST BELIEVE

If you put your trust in God.
He will help you on your way.
He will answer your needs
that you care about today.

He will make your burdens lighter
that you carry with you now,
for God alone can help you
only he can show you how.

With faith to lead you on,
you will never go astray.
Obstacles are met easily.
There is sunshine in your day

Love and worship the Lord
with each breath you breathe,
For a life full of goodness
is for those who just believe.

WHY WE SUFFER

Lord, people are evil
on this land today.
If they listen to your voice,
you will have plenty to say.

There is sickness and death,
no matter where we turn.
The devil says I have you,
but Jesus says, "when will they learn."

We often take life for granted
because we are to blind to see
when Jesus gave his life
our souls were set free.

No matter what we are going through
or what we have to face,
Jesus says, I love you
and put the devil in his place.

TIME ISN'T LONG

Time isn't long
on this earth today
Jesus says, don't worry my child
I'll guide you along the way.

When your heart is filled with pain
and it seems you can't make it through,
fall on your knees
because Jesus is waiting on you.

Life is never easy, nor is it fair.
No matter what you are going through,
the master is there.

Yes, you will get lonely
as the days go by.
Jesus says I'm with you
there's no need to cry.

Trust in him each and everyday.
No matter what the devil says to you,
it's God word we must obey.

THE FLOWER

You're the flower in my life
and you know this is true.
My life would be lost
if I couldn't be with you.

Your smile brightens the earth
and God's love calms the sea.
I just want to say thank you
because you're everything to me.

When I look in your eyes
and don't have nothing to say,
I say, Lord I love her
each and everyday.

Thank you for gracing my life.
No words can't express...
Jesus knows how I feel,
because he gave me his best.

THE SOUL

Lord, our soul is valuable
in our body you gave.
You can't put it with a price.
That's why we need to be save.

The devil wants to steal your life.
He doesn't care anything about you.
The closer we get to Jesus,
the closer we will know what to do.

Jesus, when you shed your blood
for our souls on the hill,
all the devils and his eyes,
they had to be still.

Thank you for what have done.
We wouldn't be save
if it wasn't for your son
And the life that he gave.

GOD'S WRATH

The world is ending soon.
There's no place to hide.
Jesus loves you,
so put away your pride.

Jesus' wrath is real
each and everyday.
When you hear God's voice,
get on your knees and pray.

When we read his word,
the devil won't have words to say.
Jesus you are all I have
in this sinful world today.

Tomorrow is not promised,
no matter how we plan.
If we want to get to heaven,
we must obey his command.

DIANE, DIANE

The day I met you
my life was blown away.
Jesus says, "She's the one,
and everything is ok."

I never had an angel
who made my life complete,
but God says, "Love her,"
then our love became butter sweet.

The Lord knows I love her,
she touched my soul one day.
Jesus says, "What's wrong?
She's in your life to stay."

When I look in your eyes,
there is so much to see.
Lord I love her so,
for she is a mystery.

Jesus, she changed my life.
There's no words to say.
Lord I want to thank you
for bringing her in my life one day.

She's the jewel of my life
and the apple of my heart.
Lord I want to thank you.
My love will never part

THE PRICE HE PAID

Father, your son paid the price
on the cross one day.
Many souls were lost,
but Jesus said, "No, I am the way."

Jesus, you suffered and died,
that's one thing that's true.
When they pierced you in the side,
I said hard, what does he have to go through?

They laughed at you and poked fun too,
but you said, "Father forgive them,
for they no not what they do."

Jesus, thank you for what you have done.
Our souls would have been lost
if you had not paid the cost.

THERE'S HOPE

Lord, when I came to this field
and stop and pray,
I bow down
and thank you for another day.

Jesus, when I walk along
this narrow way,
Lord, will you please
teach me how to pray?

Father, sometimes I get
lonely, sad and blue.
Without you,
I don't know what I'll do.

Remember when I'm taking
a step, maybe two or three,
I'm glad to know
you'll set me free.

THE MOMENT

Father, we live in the moment
in this world today.
The devil is busy.
That's why he has to pay.

Life is too precious
and so uncertain.
Jesus says live,
but the devil wants to pull the curtain.

Our father gave us power.
There's no time to play.
The enemy is real,
so we must pray.

Don't live for tomorrow.
Strive for today.
God is our father.
It's he we must obey

THE TEST

Father thank you for your son
because he is the best.
Lord we couldn't go on
If it wasn't for your test.

Lord sometimes we don't know
what to do
or what to blame.
The things they say about you,
it's a pity and a shame.

Jesus, you gave me strength
to fight everyday.
Your words aare powerful.
That's why the devil has to stray.

Thank you for the test.
It has really brought me near.
Because of your word and love,
I have nothing to fear.

THE WAY

Deep into the night,
Lord what do I see?
I feel your eyes
shining brightly on me.

Sometimes I'm worry
and begin to cry.
Jesus I know you are there,
because I can feel you
standing by.

When the sun is shining
on the earth so bright.
I fall on my knees
and know everything is alright.

When problems in my life
has turn over and spill.
Remember one thing:
Jesus dies on Golgotha hill.

THE LONELY DAYS

Lord there are lonely days
in my life.
I just don't understand.
It gets lonely sometimes.
Will you please take my hand?

My burdens are heavy,
and loads are to much to bear.
I get so scared at times.
Will you guide me in prayer?

People are dying everyday.
That one thing is clear.
if they fall on their knees
I know you'll be near.

So when you feel alone,
and sometimes you do,
call on the One
whose love will shine on you.

THE CROSS

Jesus you died on the cross
for our sins one day.
If it wasn't for you,
there would be no way.

You suffered on the cross.
What pain you must have felt.
People are still sinning.
I wonder do you cry,
but father does it help?

I'm glad you died for our sins,
because there was no way out.
People say they know you,
but many have their doubts.

Thank you for what you have done.
Can't no words express
what you done for our souls,
we will be eternally blessed.

GOD'S GRACE

When we walk on this earth,
there's plenty to fear.
God says "What's wrong my child?
For I am always here."

Times are getting hard,
and it seems there no end.
God said, "I love you
for it was my son, for I will help you win."

Don't take life for granted.
That's one thing you can't do.
Jesus says "Why do you fear?
For I am waiting on you."

God wakes us up in the morning
and put us to sleep at night.
The devil tries to attack you.
Jesus says "No, this is my fight."

BEAUTIFUL WITHIN

When God looks in your soul,
what does he see?
Are you really happy,
or just pretending to be?

Your heart is special
because it came from above.
The devil tries to darken it,
but God fills it with his love.

Don't let problems in your life
burden you down.
Just remember Jesus is there,
for He's always around.

When you are hurting from within,
and you are full of pain,
God knows how you feel,
for Jesus did the same.

Life is precious on this earth,
and we can't take it for granted.

In Loving Memory
of New Town, Connecticut

There is a town called New Town
that You made from above.
All the children love it
because they shared their love.

Lord, their life was cut short
on earth that they spent.
God had a son,
for they knew how Jesus went.

The children touched our lives
in a way we can't explain.
In our heart and soul,
they will always remain.

Their parents' hearts are empty,
and we know this is true.
Lord, let them know you are the only one
who can guide them through.

The children are in heaven and
we will miss them.
But we must remember God's love and He
will always surround you.

THE JOURNEY

There's times in our lives
we don't know what to do.
If we fall on our knees,
Jesus will see us through.

The road you are traveling,
It's not easy, this is true.
Don't give up,
because God's arms are around you.

When you face a challenge
and your heart is full of fear,
don't you worry about anything
for Jesus is near.

Times will get hard
with everything you face.
Just remember His love,
His mercy, and His grace.

Don't you worry about
what people say.
Know that Jesus
will guide you along the way.

Don't worry about tomorrow.
Live for today,
and what God has for you.
It can't be taken away,

Stay strong in the Lord.
It's not hard to do,
because He shed His blood
on calvary for you.

THE LONELY HEART

Lord, my heart is lonely
and filled with pain.
I fall on my knees.
Will you pick me up again?

My loads are heavy
and my burdens are light.
Please, give me the strength, to fight.

God I love you.
You're everything I need.
I can't thank you enough
for giving us your speed.

Jesus, the smile on your face,
it's such a glow.
The demons in hell, they have to go.

I can't make it without you.
I don't know where to turn.
The closer I'm with you, the more I want to learn.

So I thank you
for what you have done.
Can't no words express,
my life and heart is full,
cause you're truly the best.

SUNSHINE

When I look at your eyes,
my heart stand still.
I feel your touch.
Lord sometimes it doesn't seems real.

She's a flower in my life
that gives me a glow.
Jesus where did she come from?
Doesn't anybody know?

Lord, she's soft as cotton,
as a baby seal.
Sometimes I wonder
if her love is real.

Thank you for bringing her in my life.
She's beautiful as can be.
I love her dearly,
for she is precious to me

THE DEVIL IS A LIE

When you are sick in your body
and it won't never end,
go into prayer,
but it is Jesus who can mend.

The devil is after you.
We know it is true.
You are not alone,
because God is fighting too.

He'll hinder and hold our blessings
each and everyday.
When he think he won,
but God says no way.

When we get sick in our bodies
and the devil think he's won,
just close your eyes
and pray to the Son.

So when things are going wrong
and you begin to cry,
Just stop and think that
the devil is a lie.

QUIET TIME

Savor the time I spend with you.
It is wonderful as you can see.
How I thank you for your son, Jesus.

You brought me in this world
in our time of need.
We can't praise you enough,
for you're giving us your seed.

HIGHWAY OF LOVE

I saw Jesus walking
on the road one day.
I was lost, Jesus said, "Don't worry my child.
I'll lead the way."

When your loads are heavy
and your burdens are light,
Jesus is the one
who will carry you through the night.

The Lord made us in his image
as you can planly see.
He proved his love
out on the cross called calvery.

Jesus loves you
because everyday is bless.
Our bodies must be clean
and our sins we must confess.

When Jesus walked the earth,
it was truly a mess.
He said, "Don't worry my children,
for I will certainly bless."

Nothing can compare to His love
for I know life is a test.
Call on Him everyday,
for He will surely bless.

When you're down and out
and you can't go on,
Fall on your knees.
Jesus will make you strong.

Remember, the Lord loves you
each and everyday.
Without him,
there would be no way

THE ROAD OF LIFE

When I look at the trees
that stand across the field,
Lord sometimes I don't know
what seems to be real.

As I think about heaven,
so high above,
Lord thank you for your
sweet, undying love.

When things are blue
and doesn't go your way,
just close your eyes and thank Him
for another day.

So, when you are walking down the road
and it seems no one cares,
Remember one thing:
Jesus, is always there.

THE TREASURE

The day I met you,
My mind was blown away.
I thought I was dreaming,
but Jesus said,
"Have patience, just wait and pray."

You are beautiful flower,
which others can't compete.
Every time I get near you,
my heart skips a beat.

You have been through a lot,
and you know this is true,
for God is the one
who has been carrying you.

When you feel alone
and you think no one cares,
just look over your shoulder,
for I have always been right there.

Life is too short
and are passing away.
When God sends you someone,
treasure them every day.

I will always be here for you,
no matter how you feel.
The love I have in my heart,
it is so very real.

THE VALLEY

When I'm down and out and
it seems no one cares,
Father I know
you will be right there.

When troubles come my way
and I don't know what to do,
I ask the Lord to help me,
and he always see me through.

It seems I am in a hole
and there no way out.
I cry out to Jesus
and He hears my shout.

So when I'm down and out
and it seems I can't fight,
I call on Jesus
He is my guiding light.

PROBLEMS YOU FACE

When situations that you face
seem so hard to bear,
Don't give up because
Jesus always cares.

If things in your life seem
to go wrong,
just have faith, just believe,
just carry on.

If you call on him
and never doubt,
just pray to the Lord, He will
surely bring you out.

So remember when you pray
from your heart, soul and mind,
and when your at your roads end,
remember Jesus will always be your friend.

DON'T LOSE YOUR SOUL TO THE DEVIL

The life that we live
can be taken away.
If it wasn't for Jesus,
there wouldn't be time to pray.

The world is coming to an end.
Where are you going to go?
If your life isn't with Jesus,
there will be much pain, misery and sorrow,

Things on this earth,
they are fine in their place.
Lord that why we thank you
for your love mercy and grace.

Put your hand in the Lord's hand
and you will never go wrong.
When the enemy comes around you,
the Lord will help you to be strong.

Your soul is priceless.
Cherish it everyday,
because if the devil has it,
then it's to late to pray.

In Loving Memory of Steven A. Chesser

There was a boy name Steven
who you made from above.
All the children knew him
because they shared their love.

Lord his life was cut short
on earth that he spent.
Mary had a son,
for she knew how Jesus went.

Steven touched our lives
in a way we can't explain.
In our heart and soul,
He will always remain.

His parents' hearts are empty,
and we know this is true.
Lord, let them know you're the only one
who can guide them through.

Steven is in heaven.
We miss him, yes we do,
but remember, when God gave Jesus strength,
He'll be there for you.

THE GATHERING

Lord you called us together
for us to pray.
At first we had our doubts
but you made the way.

I was scared as could be.
You knew the reason why.
You said, "Go on
and I gave it a try."

You bless our homes.
It was simple as could be.
I got down on my knees,
then everyone was set free.

Thank you for what you have done.
It is truly the best.
If it wasn't for you,
I couldn't stand the test.

If it wasn't for the word,
I wouldn't know what to do.
But you said, "Keep trying.
I'll see you though."

Sometimes our faith got weary,
and it seemed I was alone.
You said, "I love you,
have faith, just carry on over."

So thank you Lord,
for what you have done.
No words can express...
Jesus I love you,
for you truly the best.

LORD, WHICH WAY TO GO?

Jesus is our guide
in this life we live today.
Don't worry about nothing,
because He has paved the way.

When you are all confused
sometimes you can't even pray.
Jesus says, "What's wrong?
I'll show you the way."

God is watching over you.
It may not seem like He is there.
Don't fret my child,
for you are in my arms, my love and care.

Don't you worry about
what people may say or do.
Know that Jesus is in heaven
for His word will comfort you.

THE PRESENT

The reason I'm here
because Jesus made the way.
Sometimes it gets hard.
That's why we have to pray.

No matter what you are going through,
you don't have to be alone.
Jesus died for you
upon calvery's throne.

The devil is busy.
He's plotting every day.
But Jesus says, "Pray on my child,
For he doesn't have long to stay."

Life is short
in this world today.
When you died on the cross
you made the way.

GOD'S LOVE

When it is dark in your life
and it seems you can't go through,
have faith and believe,
because God is waiting on you.

Your heart is filled with pain
and it won't come to an end.
Jesus says, "Pray on my child,
for I'm the only one who can mend."

As the days go by
and everything is dark and still,
Jesus loves you,
for he knows how you feel.

Yes, Jesus knows how you feel,
and he suffered too.
If God gave Him strength,
He'll do the same for you.

THE LONELY SOUL

Jesus loves us.
He proves it every day.
When he wakes us in the morning,
there is so much we can say

There is heart ache in our lives,
and there's one place
we don't want to go.
Jesus, you are our everything,
because we love you so.

Satan, time is ending
on this earth today.

THE HILL WHICH COMETH MY HELP

Deep in the valley,
Lord what do I see?
Situations are hard.
The enemy is all around me.

Every time I try to run,
there's no place to go.
God, when I'm in trouble,
Lord you are with me so.

When things in life seems
so very hard,
and you just don't understand,
just know God is the master
and has everything in His hand.

When you look in the sky
in the heavens above,
just remember one thing:
God always shares his love.

THE TRUE FRIEND

There are no words to describe you.
You are beautiful as can be.
Jesus knows how I feel because
you are everything to me.

You are a diamond in my life,
the jewel of my soul.
My heart is in a million pieces.
Only you can make it whole.

When the sun shines in the day
and the rain falls at night,
I ask the Lord, "Where is she?
Is everything alright?"

You a jewel on this earth
that I see every day.
I don't know what I would do
Lord, if you went away.

You are an angel in my life
that I love so dear.
Lord, I want to thank you
for bringing her here.

Jesus' Love

Nothing on this earth
can compare to His love.
The devil tries to stop it,
but it comes from above.

When troubles in your life
seems so hard to bear,
Jesus says, "This is my child,
for I am always there."

People are suffering
in this world today.
The devil thinks he was won
But God says no, "He can not stay."

Jesus you wake us up,
which you don't have to do.
Lord, if we didn't have you,
what would we go through?

Sometimes our hearts get heavy
and you think you can't take it.
If Jesus is walking by your side,
then you know you can make it.

THE HEART WITHIN

Sometimes it's dark in your heart,
and you don't know what to do.
If you search your soul,
God has an answer for you.

When you look within your soul,
there is nothing to see.
The devil, says he has you,
but God says no,
"Get on your knees and pray to me,"

The devil puts darkness your heart
so you won't be able to pray,
but if you read God's word,
all doubts will go away.

So stay strong in the Lord,
no matter what you do.
Jesus is on the throne,
sitting there waiting on you.

FEAR

When you have a problem
and can't solve it alone,
look up to heaven
and know that God is on the throne.

Sometimes we get scared
and sometimes we fear,
but remember one thing:
Jesus is always near.

Don't worry about tomorrow,
only today.
Just know the Lord
has made the way.

So when life gets you down
and it seems you can't win,
just remember Jesus
will be there to the end.

THE BROKEN HEART

Lord will you mend this broken heart?
My life seems as if it's at an end.
Jesus says, "I love you,
for I will pick you up again."

No matter what you are
going through
or what you may have to face,
God will put them in their place

Your heart is full of pain
and you don't know what to do.
Fall on your knees
cause Jesus did the same thing, too.

Yes, your heart is filled with pain
and the devil is not through.
God is our master
but Jesus is waiting on you.

WHEN GOD SENDS YOU SOMEONE

When Jesus came on this earth,
He knew what he had to do.
the devil got busy,
but God saw him through.

People live on this earth
and they take matters in their own hands.
Who are you going to listen to?
The devil's voice or God's command?

When God sends you someone,
He gives you the best.
The devil is listening,
but God will do the rest.

When you love someone
and they let you go,
God says, "These are my children.
Yes are they lonely,
but I love them so."

Remember, God knows who you need
just know you are never alone.
Jesus knows how you feel,
cause he died upon the throne.

THE WOMAN I LOVE

Her name is Diane.
She is the flower in my life.
When God told me about her,
I thought she was going to be my wife.

She is beautiful as can be,
an angel on this planet,
but the devil came in,
and she took us for granted.

I will never love a woman
on this earth that we live.
God knew I love her,
but father help me to forgive.

Diane is a special woman,
and she's very unique.
Just to look in her eyes,
she made my life complete.

I don't know what went wrong
or what happen that day.
God said son, "Just get on your
knees trust me and pray."

Diane, I will always love you
no matter what you say.
In time, our hearts
will bring us back one day.

FREEDOM

Jesus I know you died
for my soul one day.
If it wasn't for you,
there wouldn't be no way.

Sometimes my heart gets heavy.
It seems like there's no end,
but I remember one thing:
You are truly my friend.

Yes you get lonely
and don't know what to do,
I lift my hands,
and know you'll see me through.

When my soul gets burdened,
and I have many doubts,
Jesus you're the one
who will bring me out.

ABOUT THE AUTHOR

Greg E. Steppes, a native of Los Angeles, California has been writing inspirational poetry since the 1980s. He is the son of Gloria and Ted Steppes and is the oldest of four sisters and five brothers. An active member of the community, Greg describes himself as an usher, gardener, writer, and prayer warrior. Professionally, he is a CNA and volunteers with a local ambulance company. He currently lives in Ruston, Louisiana, where he has resided since 1978.